# Easyway Guides

# Guide To Writing a C.V. And Conducting a Successful Interview The Easyway

HOWARD ROGERS

Easyway Guides

Easyway Guides
Brighton BN2 4EG

© Straightforward Publishing 2010

British Library Cataloguing in Publication data. A catalogue record for
this book is available from the British Library.

9781847161765

Printed in Great Britain by GN Digital Books Essex

Cover design by Bookworks Islington

# CONTENTS

## The complete CV

**Covering Letters**

**Application Forms**

## Other tips

## Interviews

# Introduction

The main objective of this book is to demonstrate the most effective way of formulating the ideal CV. The current job climate in this country is bleak, with more cuts to come. Certainly, the job market will become more competitive than it already is and more people will be chasing fewer jobs than ever. That's why formulating a CV that stands out from the rest is essential, particularly at this moment in time.

Certainly, the way we initially present ourselves to a prospective employer is very important and can mean the difference between getting a job we want and failing. Presenting ourselves begins with the CV. This is the very first contact that an employer will have with us.

*Although many people know the basics of putting a CV together, there is a big difference between those who have studied the technique and those who have not.*

Many applicants undersell themselves right at the outset with a poorly laid out CV that contains too little information. The purpose of this book is to enable those who read it to ensure that the best possible CV is formulated, a CV which shows the applicant in the best light and which provides a stepping stone to the all important interview.

*Your CV won't actually get you a job!*

This happens at the interview stage. It will, however, get you through the door and put you in the race. Because your CV is so important it is obvious that it should be as neat as possible, presented on good quality paper and accurate in all respects. Remember that your CV is being looked at cold by someone who has never met you and therefore first impressions count for everything.

The book assumes that you will be applying for jobs within the United Kingdom. If this is not the case, you must research the company even more thoroughly and fall in with local customs. For example, in some countries of the world, it is customary to tell the employer in what high esteem you hold them and that you want this particular job more than any other job. This approach would not be acceptable in the UK.

The overall approach this book takes is to build up an effective CV as it progresses. It also offers advice to the job hunter in such areas as writing the ideal covering letter and also how to construct particular types of CVs depending on your circumstances. application forms, which many firms still insist on, sending your CV ensuring it gets maximum exposure and tips on making it computer friendly are also dealt with.

Throughout this book the masculine gender has been used for ease. However, obviously the information is for male and female alike.

Good luck in your job hunting!

# Interpreting Adverts

# 1

## Understanding Advertisements

If you are sending your CV in response to a job advert, then understanding the job advertisement is the key to designing an effective Curriculum Vitae. Your CV needs to be formulated with that specific job in mind and it is of fundamental importance that you are able to interpret and analyze the advertisement and make correct deductions. If you do not, then your CV will miss the point and you may not progress to the next stage.

### How the job is described

All advertisements will tell the reader the name, location and business of the company. These will be put across in a positive way. Next will come the description. Take time to think about how the job is described. This will enable you to get a real idea of what the company is after. Look to see whether you will be working alone or in a team. This is very important, particularly when emphasizing skills and experience on your CV.

The company will describe what they do, what they require, then go on to outline qualifications and experience required.

Obviously, this is one of the most important areas of the advertisement and should be read with care and clearly understood. In some cases, qualifications and experience required will be clearly stated. However, in other cases they won't and it will be up to you to infer these from the advert, based on your knowledge of the job.

## Salary

Although, as described above, the salary attached to a job can be misleading, in many cases the actual salary to be offered is not quoted. Statements such as "attractive salary package" or "salary commensurate with age and experience" are employed. The rule here is that if a salary is very attractive it will be quoted. Look at what is said about the salary. The word "circa" may mean 'around' but quite often read by potential applicants as a minimum.

Many advertisements, particularly for posts in the public sector, give salary ranges. This shows interested applicants what their potential would be as well as the starting salary. Most organizations will negotiate the starting salary after they have made a decision to employ someone.

## Company description and philosophy

Look at what the company has to say for itself. This usually tells you how it wants to perceive itself rather than how others see it. The company may state that it is expanding, or might give that impression by advertising for a number of positions. You might get an idea of the possible promotion prospects from the advertisement. Be wary if there is a lack of company description. This does not always mean that there is a problem, the company may be huge and well known, therefore an in-depth description is not necessary. However, there may well be a flip side and the company may have something to hide, such as concealing recruitment information from other staff.

On company philosophy, look for equal opportunities statements etc. These vary enormously, with the public sector generally leading the way. You need to consider how important the existence of an equal opportunities statement is for you.

## Media used to advertise position

The medium used to advertise the post can tell you a lot. If an advertisement is in a national paper then it usually means that the employer has decided that they will spend more money in order to cast their net wider, i.e., nationally instead of locally. Some companies use agencies. This means that they have chosen to have the screening done by another party. In this case, it will be your job to convince the agency that they should introduce you to the company. Sometimes, the agency carries out initial interviews and only submits the short list to their client. You may want to consider making your application more general if the agency handles many jobs in the industry in which you work. Think about the reasons why the organizations use agencies. Do they want specialists for whom that agency is known? Do they not have much expertise in that area themselves? This can be true when companies are seeking personnel at the top of a department, where there is nobody above with the kind of knowledge required to recruit that person.

Good advertisements are not only the right size but are also the right shape too. They have usually been professionally designed to attract the reader to the text, demonstrating careful planning and thought. Not all organizations can afford this approach. Look for simple indicators too, i.e., is the advertisement boxed? Lineage advertisements in local papers may tell you that the company is small and unsophisticated in terms of recruitment. Look at how accurately the job is described - beware of those sounding too good to be true, few jobs live up to this.

The above are key things to look out for when reading a job advertisement. Remember, read the advertisement carefully; concentrate on each aspect building up a picture as you go. If you are in any doubt, contact the company advertising the job and request further information.

*Now read the key points from Chapter One.*

# KEY POINTS FROM CHAPTER ONE

- Pay careful attention to the job description in the advertisement. This will enable you to get a clear idea of what the company wants.

- Most organizations will negotiate the starting salary after they have made a decision to employ someone

- Read the company description carefully and try to determine the company philosophy

- The medium used by the organization to advertise the post will tell you a lot about the organization

- If the company uses an agency, you may want to structure your CV a little differently.

# Compiling Your CV

# 2

## Putting Together a CV

Having either decided to send out your CV to various employers or websites, or CV banks (see later) or examined and analyzed a job advertised, you should now be in a position to begin constructing your CV.

### Fundamental requirements of a CV

The letters "CV" stand for Curriculum Vitae, which derives from Latin. Translated, this means "the way your life has run". Correspondingly, the CV is a personal statement, which demonstrates to the employer the way your life has run. The CV will usually start from your early education and progress through to higher education and chronicle your employment. It will also chronicle your personal interests. The end product should present a well-rounded picture of you.

A CV serves several basic requirements. Firstly, it highlights your potential value to an employer. It also provides a framework within which an interview can be guided and acts as a record of the interview, or its substance.

Many people suffer mental blocks when required to formulate a CV. It can be hard work. Time and effort plus creativity are key components of the task. The most important point to remember at the outset is that the CV should be concise and easy to read. All of the relevant and most important facts should be present.

## The layout of the ideal CV

Before any information has been entered onto the CV, consideration needs to be given to the layout. By layout, I mean the actual design of the visual presentation. Remember that a better impression will be made if the person reading the CV feels comfortable with what they are reading. Effective visual design reflects neatness, and the end product should be easy on the eyes and immediately give an impression of orderliness, which will go a long way to impress the reader.

Chapter Seven gives two examples of complete CV's laid out in a simple but effective manner.

Although final recruitment decisions are not made on visual presentation alone, as opposed to content, the way information is assembled makes an important first impression and could mean the difference between someone bothering to spend time with your CV or deciding to move on to the next one.

Make sure also when you are typing the information that you use all of the features of the Word Processor (assuming that you are using a WP). Make sure that you have clean margins and that you are consistent when presenting your information. For example, you might want to ensure that your work is not right hand justified as this lends a certain uniformity to a CV. Maybe it is better to leave it unjustified or "ragged right" as it is known.

## Quality

Obviously the quality of a CV depends very much on the way it is laid out and the information contained within it. However, it is also true to say that a much better impression is made with a quality paper. There are different qualities and thickness of paper and I would recommend that a thicker more durable paper be used, such as Conqueror. A good quality paper at the outset enhances the effort that you will make when laying out information and presenting yourself in the best light.

## Style

By style, I am referring to the way you present information about yourself. Remember that there are two important rules underlying any form of presentation

Be brief and be clear! You do not want to bore the reader by going on and on, using twenty words when five will do. However, conversely, you do not want to be too brief and exclude the main emphasis of what you wish to get across.

Writing the ideal CV is a skilled business and requires thought and concentration, along with creative editing. If possible, I would advise showing the finished product to someone skilled in the art of report writing before you send it to a prospective employer. As we progress through the book there will be examples of the kind of style you should be aiming for. These examples will build up into a complete CV, which should set the standard you are trying to achieve.

## The basic structure

Although the basic structure of a CV is well known, it is more important to structure the CV in a way that shows you in the best light.

**The traditional structure of a CV is as follows (see overleaf):**

Name
Address
Occupation
Telephone number (landline and mobile)
Email
Date of birth
Place of birth
Marital status
Next of kin
Health
Driving license
Religion (if applicable)
National insurance number
(Sometimes religion, nationality and passport number if applying for a job abroad)
Secondary education
Higher education
Professional qualifications
Employment history
Other (interests, achievements etc.)

There are several variants on this approach. Remember, what you are doing is delivering information to the potential employer. This person might well be interested in your employment history at the outset and it may be more effective to deliver this information right at the beginning. Leave the matter of details such as date of birth and secondary education until the end and begin with the most important first. Therefore, instead of adopting the traditional approach you might want to use the following format:

Name
Address
Telephone number
Email
Career
Achievements
Professional qualifications
Education
Interests
Other personal details
Date of birth

We have considered the most important aspects of the ideal CV. These are quality, style and layout. Finally, there is the content. These initial pointers should enable you to begin to put together your first CV. In the following chapter we will look at the presentation of your personal details and how to obtain the ideal structure. It is important to remember that I will be following the traditional format when presenting each area of information. It will be up to yourself to rearrange the format as you think best.

*Now please read the key points from Chapter Two overleaf.*

# KEY POINTS FROM CHAPTER TWO
# DESIGNING THE IDEAL CV

- Your CV should always present a well-rounded, balanced picture of you as a person.

- Your CV highlights your potential value to an employer. It should be concise and easy to read

- Your CV should be well laid out. Visual presentation is of the utmost importance

- Use good quality paper when producing your CV.

- Be brief and clear when outlining the various areas of your CV.

- Use a tried and tested format. There are several variations outlined in this book.

# 3

## Personal Details

The approach from hereon in is to build up a complete CV, with each chapter concentrating on a specific area.

As I stated in Chapter Two, personal details do not necessarily come first in your CV but the arrangements of this section are similar in all CVs. The only differences relate to the amount of information given and where it appears. The most obvious information you should open with is that of your name and address and telephone number. You should also put your occupation.

### Date of birth and place of birth

If the CV is being assembled for a single job application then the applicant's age should appear alongside the date of birth. This reduces the reading time of the CV. When the CV is to be used over a long period then the date of birth should be inserted because the passage of time will lead to inaccuracy. The entry giving details about ages of children can also become outdated and therefore it is important to supply date of birth here too. In addition to date of birth, place of birth should be entered too. Interestingly, many public sector employers now do not ask for date of birth on application forms, as the feeling is that this may lead to indirect discrimination when picking a candidate. However, it is the norm to do so on CV's.

## Nationality

Depending on what post you are applying for, and where in the world, you should refer to nationality. If the job is in the United Kingdom, this is not strictly necessary.

## Religion

Again, you should only make reference to religion if it is relevant. For most job applications, it is not necessary. For jobs abroad where it is deemed to be of importance you should state your religion.

## Marital status

Make reference to whether you are married or single. It is not really necessary to allude to the fact that you are separated or divorced.

## Next of kin

Next of kin should be entered as a matter of course, particularly if the nature and type of work is dangerous.

## Passport number

You should make reference to this if the post is abroad. Otherwise it is not necessary.

## Health

Another sub heading which may not be used in all instances is that of health. This will apply if physical fitness is an important consideration, jobs such as swimming instructor, physical fitness trainer etc.

## Driving license

Details concerning your driving license can be important. A potential employer may be impressed by a clean license. If the license is not clean then you should indicate that you have a full license only.

## Relocation

If you wish it to be known that you would be prepared to relocate to another part of the country then you should indicate this.

You may not want to be specific here, therefore leaving open the question of relocation.

# National insurance number

Your national insurance number should always be included in your personal details. This is particularly relevant when the CV is being used to apply for a job offshore. You should know your own field of work and when to include this information.

Personal details should be presented as in the example below. You may not require all of the information outlined. However, it is important to remember that you are tailoring your details to the potential employer. Obviously, some of the details will be wholly dependent on your prospective employer.

---

PERSONAL DETAILS

Full Name:         Rupert James
Occupation:       Computer Scientist
Address:           92 Faversham Street Weybridge Surrey
Telephone Number: 01239 6789
Mobile 98767545321
Email info@straightforwardco.co.uk
Date of Birth:      5-3-75
Place of Birth:     Rich Street Ninetown Anywhere
Nationality:       British
Religion:          Buddhist
Marital Status:    Married with son aged 7
Next of Kin:       Mrs. James address as above

---

| | |
|---|---|
| National ins no: | 123456789 |
| Driving License: | Current full |
| Passport Number: | 456789 |
| Health: | Excellent |
| Preferred location: | Anywhere at all |

The personal details section of the CV is straightforward. The most important point to remember is that apart from the obvious information, such as name and address there are important areas which are directly relevant to the job for which you are applying and which you must include.

*Now please read the key points from Chapter Three overleaf.*

# KEY POINTS FROM CHAPTER THREE
# PRESENTATION OF PERSONAL DETAILS

- Your personal details may vary according to the post offered

- If your CV is being assembled for a single job application, mention your age. For multiple applications mention your date of birth

- Don't forget to include your name and address. Many people do!

# 4

# Education
# Qualifications And Training

Obviously, education, qualifications and training will differ according to individual experience. Normally, in a CV you would include education from the age of eleven onwards. It is not necessary to include schools attended prior to secondary schools. Sometimes a person will have attended more than one secondary school, for a variety of reasons, such as parents moving job, and in this case you should normally only include the last two schools.

Your achievements at school, in the form of GCSE should be clearly demonstrated. You might wish to emphasize the most relevant passes first although it is usual to rank the passes in descending order.

*Example*
JULY 1991
GCSE

| | | |
|---------|-------|-----|
| English | Grade | (d) |
| Biology | | (c) |
| French | | (c) |
| Physics | | (c) |

Economics                              (a)

And so on.

## Higher Education

For those who have received an education after leaving secondary school, whether it is university or technical college, it is usual to present the nature and type of education and your qualifications. For those who left school and went straight into employment with no formal qualifications it is usual to proceed with your career history.

If you have gone on to higher education then the next stage of the CV will look something like this:

September 1993 - July 1996          Waldesley Polytechnic High Street Waldesley

Subject BA Computer Sciences
Grade   2.1

If your further education has been more technically oriented, i.e., part time day release, then the entry would look more like this:

September 1993 - September 1996 City and Guilds
Subject                              Computer Science Part 1

Grade                                    Pass

September 1997 - September 1998        City and Guilds
Subject                                  Computer Science Part 2
Grade                                    Pass with merit

The above is only an example and does not relate to the actual computing syllabus. It could be that you have attained a number of qualifications during your time at university or college and that you have a long list of diplomas or certificates. The question to consider here is whether or not to include them all or whether to stick to the relevant ones.

The employer would first and foremost be interested in the qualification, which is most relevant to the job being applied for. Then the focus would be on the relevant areas of practical experience underpinning the paper qualification.

Although you may have obtained numerous certificates or diplomas in other subjects, which may well be an indication of intelligence, self-discipline and determination, it is really the most relevant qualification, which is the most important.

The key point to remember is that information overload may serve as a distraction and draw the potential employer's attention away from the most important qualification.

## Placements during training

Placements with other organizations, such as industrial placements or college placements, whatever the length should be treated as a normal job in the career history, with the placement clearly emphasized:

*Example*
October 1993 - April 1994.      Finetronics Ltd, Long Road, Waldesley.
Computer Trainee - Assisting the Chief Engineer
on placement developing computer systems

## Short courses

Over the years an applicant will have attended many short courses either connected with his employment or voluntarily. You should only really make reference to short courses if they have relevance to the job being applied for. Again it is no use entering a proliferation of courses attended if all you are achieving is information overload.

*Example*
Authentic Electronics Ltd
July (1999) Fault finding on Computers (2 days)
September (1999)      Software Analysis
December (1999)      Advanced Spreadsheets

Sometimes recruitment agencies will rely on key words when retrieving potential candidates from databases. For example, Comp for computer specialists. If your CV is going to a particular agency it is a good idea to ensure that you are aware of the need to insert any relevant abbreviations, which might be used as key words

.

## Professional Associations

It is at this point, at the end of your formal qualifications and before your career history, that you would insert your professional qualifications, if any. Professional qualifications, in most cases, are obtained following a specialist course and then after a period in the relevant job. A professional qualification is intended to demonstrate that you have received the appropriate amount of academic and practical training and that you are a competent person able to operate in your given field. Therefore, the entry might look like this:

Professional Association: Royal Institution of Computer Technicians. Date entered: October 1998

If you think it is relevant, you might consider using the letters relating to your profession alongside your name when entering your personal details. The same consideration might also be given to Educational qualifications, i.e., BA (hons).

## Service in the Armed Forces

If you have served in the Armed Forces then your education within the military will be emphasized in exactly the same way as the previous example. The potential employer will see at a glance that you were in the forces and will expect to see this in your career history.

See overleaf

# Education, Training and Qualifications

Building up on what we have included so far, this section of your CV should look as follows:

Education:   1986 - 1993
Northampton Grammar School
GCE Passes:

| | |
|---|---|
| English | Grade (d) |
| Biology | (c) |
| French | (c) |
| Physics | (b) |
| Economics | (b) |

## Higher Education

1993-1996 Waldesley Polytechnic, High Street, Waldesley
Northampton
BA   Computer Sciences: Pass with distinction
Year One:   Computer Theory
Year Two:   Advanced Computer Theory
"      "        Computer Trainee on placement,
ElectronicsSystems Ltd, Long Road, Northampton. Assisting the Chief Engineer developing computer systems

Year Three:  Applied Computing

## Short Courses

Authentic Electronics Limited
July 1999              Fault-finding on Computers  (2 days)

September 1999     Software Analysis (1 week)

December 1999     Advanced Spreadsheets (1 week)

**Professional Association**

Royal Institute of Computers

Fellow of the Institute October 1999

*Now you should read the key points from Chapter Four overleaf.*

# KEY POINTS FROM CHAPTER FOUR
# EDUCATION, QUALIFICATIONS AND TRAINING

- Include only education from the age of eleven onwards (secondary)

- Your achievements at school should be clearly demonstrated

- Highlight higher education. Emphasize your most relevant qualifications

- Emphasize relevant short courses

- Be aware of the need to insert relevant abbreviations when sending your CV to recruitment agencies

- Highlight professional associations to which you belong

- Highlight service in the Armed Forces

# 5

## Career History

So far we have looked at personal details and your education and qualifications. However, it is true to say that it is the next part of your CV which will be of the most interest to the would-be employer.

This section, of all sections, will demand the greatest amount of time and thought, as employers will be looking to see what sort of experience you can bring to their organization. Although your education may be first class and your qualifications second to none they will almost always take second place to your actual experience in a particular field.

When producing this area of the CV (as with all areas) avoid long flowing prose and avoid the use of the first person, i.e., I \ we, as your document will only usually get a quick first reading and therefore lots of irrelevant information may put off the potential employer. Familiarity in a CV will usually go down very badly indeed so stick to the facts and be objective.

You should always begin with your current employer first (or most recent) devoting the most time and space here, as it is the one the potential employer will see as most relevant. The standard procedure is to catalogue your jobs in reverse order, showing the name and business of the employer, the dates of employment in months and years and the job and duties.

The material must be well organized in this section to enable the employer to see where your main strengths are. The exact address of the organization is not needed but is helpful to indicate the area. Some people do not name their company. This is not recommended. It gives the impression that they are ashamed of it and makes it harder for the person assessing the application to get a feel for what the individual was doing.

Many things are deduced by the reader, taking into account the job title, the company business and size and the list of your duties. These things all contribute to helping to build up a picture of the sort of work undertaken and leaving out the company name denies the reader some of that information.

You will not need to give details of the grades of your previous positions. This would be irrelevant to a new employer and in any case the recruiter is unlikely to know the details of the grading structure of your last employers. Although you may have been in a high grade, omit details of this. Ensure instead that you put in information on any promotions that you gained. You may also want to mention merit increases gained, although this may be done through the covering letter rather than the curriculum vitae.

In cases where you have undertaken a number of similar jobs, amalgamate these into one section if this is feasible. Give a brief outline of the duties with the caveat that you had similar employment in those companies and give inclusive dates.

You do not have to include reasons for leaving, or salary. However, you might want to indicate the salary for your current/last employment in order to give the prospective employer an indication of what salary you might be asking for.

**Your career history**

Taking into account the above, the section of your CV dealing with your career history would look as follows:

CAREER HISTORY

August 2004 - current.
Authentic Computers, Northampton. Consultant
In this post, I am acting in the capacity of consultant to the private and public sectors, advising on systems usage. I am employing the technical know how gained in my previous jobs. I am conversant with most computer packages

Salary: £25,000 Per Annum

September 2001 - July 2004
London Borough of Shepwhich. Senior Computer Manager

In this post, I had responsibility for overseeing a change in the authority's computer system. This involved carrying out systems analysis and producing a brief for the council, who subsequently accepted the brief and instructed the computer department to effect the change.

After two years I was promoted from Computer Manager to Senior Computer Manager.

September 1999 - August 2001
I took one year out before work to fulfill ambitions to travel around the world with my wife.

*Now read the key points from Chapter Five.*

# KEY POINTS FROM CHAPTER FIVE
# PRESENTATION OF CAREER DETAILS

- This section of your CV is the most important area of the Document

- Avoid long flowing prose. Avoid the use of the first person

- Begin with your current employer first, listing jobs in reverse order

# 6

## Additional Information

---

In addition to the main points of your C.V, you may feel that it is necessary to include other details. The following covers main areas of information that may assist the interviewer in the initial stages of the job-hunting process.

### Health

Unless you have had a serious illness that you feel a potential employer should be aware of, then it might be wise to omit this. The person scrutinizing the application will assume that you are in good health unless you state otherwise.

If you have spent time away from employment due to illness, and there is a gap in your CV. then it might be wise to explain this separately, emphasizing that there are no recurring problems and that you are fit for work.

One point worth remembering is that employers with over 20 employees are required by law (Disability Discrimination Act) to employ a quota of three per cent of disabled persons in the workplace. The Act only deals with registered disabled and is very difficult to enforce, however.

## References

Omit references unless you are specifically asked for them. Where you are asked to give references, use your most recent or current employer if possible and the one immediately prior to that. If you are applying for your first job, be prepared to use a tutor at your school or college.

Whenever you give the name of referees, ask the individuals first if they are willing to provide a reference for you.

## Salary

This is another detail that can generally be omitted, especially if your employment history spans a few years.

Payments received several decades ago are not relevant now. The employer is more interested in your most recent salary, as they will usually base their own decisions on this information. If your salary is good in your current job, you may want to leave details of this out as it may deter a potential employer of they think that they cannot match it. If your current salary is poor, the reader may wish to know why this is the case. Therefore, you may wish to leave this blank also.

## Personal Interests

You should think carefully about what you wish to include in this section. Try to tailor it to the post you are applying for. Try to list interests that show a balance. A healthy interest in sport and the outdoors should be counterbalanced by other, more intellectual pursuits. In general, keep this section short, as it is an extra, which you are adding in order to give the reader a more complete picture of you.

## Languages

You should make reference to languages that you can speak, other than your mother tongue, only if they are pertinent to the post applied for. Only give information about languages that you can speak if you really know them. It is no good embellishing the truth and being shown up at an interview.

## Other

Make reference to your driving license. Usually, employers like to see that you have a license although some jobs do not require one. If you have produced any publications that are relevant to the post, make reference to these. Generally, it is the more academically inclined jobs that feel publications are relevant.

However, other employers offering legal or advice posts might be suitably impressed if you have produced work that has been published.

Experience in the Armed Forces usually impresses employers as it denotes a person who has been subject to a life of organized discipline and would probably turn out to be a trustworthy employee. This, of course, may not always be the case, but general perceptions are most important when getting beyond the first stage.

# The Complete CV

# 7

## Examples of Complete CV's

The following are examples of two different layout styles of a CV. The information is the same and includes all elements. However, you should include and exclude information depending on the perceived requirements of the employer. For example, it may not be necessary to include religion or location or other facts. This depends entirely on the employer.

**Example 1**

PERSONAL DETAILS

| | |
|---|---|
| Full Name: | Rupert James |
| Occupation: | Computer Scientist |
| Address: | 92 Faversham Street |
| Telephone Number: | 012396789 |
| Mobile | 98767545321 |
| Email | info@straightforwardco.co.uk |
| Date of Birth: | 5-3-75 |
| Place of Birth: | Rich Street Ninetown Anywhere |
| Nationality: | British |
| Religion: | Buddhist |
| Marital Status: | Married with son aged 7 |
| Next of Kin: | Mrs James address as above |
| National ins no: | 123456789 |

Driving License:     Current full
Passport Number:   456789
Health:                   Excellent
Preferred location:   Anywhere at all


**Education, Training and Qualifications**


Education:   1986 - 1993


Northampton Grammar School
GCE Passes:

| | |
|---|---|
| English | Grade (d) |
| Biology | (c) |
| French | (c) |
| Physics | (b) |
| Economics | (b) |

**Higher Education**
1993 - 1996  Waldesley Polytechnic, High Street,
Waldesley Northampton
BA   Computer Sciences: Pass with distinction
Year One:    Computer Theory
Year Two    Advanced Computer Theory
    "           Computer Trainee on placement,
               ElectronicsSystems Ltd,
               Long Road, Northampton.
               Assisting the Chief Engineer
               developing computer systems

Year Three: Applied Computing

Short Courses
Authentic Electronics Limited September 2004 Fault finding on Computers (2days)
October 2004         Software Analysis (1 week)
December 2004         Advanced Spreadsheets (1 week)

**Professional Association**
Royal Institute of Computers
Fellow of the Institute May 2004

CAREER HISTORY

August 2004 - current.
Authentic Computers, Northampton. Consultant
In this post, I am acting in the capacity of consultant to the private and public sectors, advising on systems usage. I am employing the technical know how gained in my previous jobs.

I am conversant with most computer packages
Salary: £25,000 Per Annum
September 2001 - July 2004
London Borough of Shepwhich. Senior Computer Manager

In this post, I had responsibility for overseeing a change in the authority's computer system. This involved carrying out systems analysis and producing a brief for the council, who subsequently accepted the brief and instructed the computer department to effect the change.

After two years I was promoted from Computer Manager to Senior Computer Manager.

Whilst employed by The London Borough of Shepwhich I obtained the status of Fellow of the Royal Institute of Computer Scientists. My main duties for the company were to oversee the development of a computer system for a local authority. This involved giving technical advice to the authority and supervising a workforce of 23 people who were directly involved in the installation of the equipment. During this time, I gained experience of the following packages:

Wing 1 - Wing 2 - Super Wing-Wing for Windows

September 1999 - August 2001
I took two years out from work to fulfill ambition to travel around the world with my wife.

**Personal Interests**

I am interested in squash, badminton and indoor football. In addition, I am interested in studying history and Science. I enjoy walking in the countryside and swimming. I also like to participate in the community and am on the local conservation committee. I speak French and German fluently and have traveled to these countries for my current employer on business.

**Health**
Excellent

**Preferred location**
London

OVERLEAF FOR EXAMPLE 2

# Example 2

| | |
|---|---|
| Name | Rupert James |
| Address | 92 Faversham Street Weybridge Surrey |
| Telephone number | 020 8 1234 5678 |
| Mobile | 98767545321 |

Email info@straightforwardco.co.uk
Occupation          Computer Scientist

## Career

August 2004 - current.
Authentic Computers, Northampton. Consultant
In this post, I am acting in the capacity of consultant to the private and public sectors, advising on systems usage. I am employing the technical know how gained in my previous jobs. I am conversant with most computer packages

Salary: £25,000 Per Annum

September 2001 - July 2004

London Borough of Shepwhich. Senior Computer Manager

In this post, I had responsibility for overseeing a change in the authority's computer system. This involved carrying out systems analysis and producing a brief for the council, who subsequently accepted the brief and instructed the computer department to effect the change.

After two years I was promoted from Computer Manager to Senior Computer Manager.

Whilst employed by The London Borough of Shepwhich I obtained the status of Fellow of the Royal Institute of Computer Scientists. My main duties for the company were to oversee the development of a computer system for a local authority. This involved giving technical advice to the authority and supervising a workforce of 23 people who were directly involved in the installation of the equipment. During this time, I gained experience of the following packages:
Wing 1 - Wing 2 - Super Wing-Wing for Windows

September 1999 – August 2001
I took one year out from work to fulfill ambition to travel around the world with my wife.

## Professional Qualifications

Fellow of the Royal Institute of Computer Scientists, May 2004.

## Education, Training and Qualifications
Education:   1986 - 1993

Northampton Grammar School
GCE Passes:

| | |
|---|---|
| English | Grade (d) |
| Biology | (c) |
| French | (c) |
| Physics | (b) |
| Economics | (b) |

## Higher Education

1993 – 1996 Waldesley Polytechnic, High Street, Waldesley
Northampton
BA   Computer Sciences: Pass with distinction
Year One: Computer Theory
Year Two: Advanced Computer Theory
    "     " Computer Trainee on placement,
            Electronics Systems Ltd, Long Road, Northampton.
Assisting the Chief Engineer developing computer systems

Year Three: Applied computing

## Short Courses

Authentic Electronics Limited
September 2004 Fault finding on Computers  (2 days)
October 2004      Software Analysis (1 week)
December 2004    Advanced Spreadsheets (1 week)

## Personal Interests

I am interested in squash, badminton and indoor football. In addition, I am interested in studying history and Science. I enjoy walking in the countryside and swimming. I also like to participate in the community and am on the local conservation committee.

I speak French and German fluently and have traveled to these countries for my current employer on business.

## Other personal details

| | |
|---|---|
| Date of Birth: | 5-3-75 |
| Place of Birth: | Rich Street Ninetown Anywhere |
| Nationality: | British |
| Religion: | Buddhist |
| Marital Status: | Married with Son aged 7 |
| Next of Kin: | Mrs. Smith address as above |
| National ins no: | 012396789 |
| Driving License: | Current full |
| Passport Number: | 456789 |
| Health: | Excellent |
| Preferred location: | Anywhere at all |

The above two examples represent two different ways of laying out a CV. The information is the same but is presented in a different way. The reader will see different facts first. You must decide which will be of primary importance for this particular employer. The key point is that you are presenting what you consider to be the most important and relevant facts first.

Example one concentrated on personal details first, followed by education and career Example two-placed immediate emphasis on career then education, with personal details last.

# 8

## Different CVs

### School leavers

Most school leavers will have very little experience of the job market, with the exception of a Saturday job or evening employment. The fact that you do not have a career history to demonstrate should enable you to keep this part of your CV brief. Generally, you should aim to keep to one side of A4 paper.

Your education will be the most important part of your CV if you are a school leaver. You should try to include any work experience that you may have had. This will include work experience programmers and Youth Training Programmes.

You should list all work experience, highlighting grades achieved. If they are not too good, you should omit them. The employer can ask for details if these are needed. You will invariably have to explain the nature of the qualifications. If you are older then the school system will have changed. However, if you are about to leave school then the would-be employer may not understand your qualifications. One example is that employers are now getting used to the grading systems of the GCSE and Envy's (General National Vocational Qualifications) and would possibly be out of touch or not see the relevance of GCSE levels.

You should attempt to make a connection between your hobbies and your personal qualities, which show your skills and aptitudes. Organizational skills are generally valued and participation in voluntary work can help to create a positive image of you as a person.

Do try to avoid quoting too many interests or give the impression of being a flighty person. The employer is usually more concerned that you are able to settle into a work environment, especially as you have not experienced the world of work and the attendant discipline.

If you have been involved in the arena of student politics, be careful how you mention this. Some employers are not over keen to employ someone who they perceive may cause disruption or upset a well-established applecart. There is no harm mentioning areas of responsibility such as president of your branch of the National Union of Students, but don't go much beyond this, unless of course a prospective employer knows you and your political skills and history are an asset.

# Graduates

For those people who are just graduating, or have graduated, obviously the emphasis will be on experience at University or College. However, the whole emphasis won't be on the academic content but will also be on what you did outside of your studies, such as vacation work, gap year and so on.

What you need to illustrate is that you are self-disciplined, have goals in life and also have initiative. This is likely to get you to the interview stage in your chosen career path.

The key is to structure your CV in such a way that you start with personal details and then, after early schooling, build up the years that you were a student and bring out all aspects of your experience and use this to justify your choice of job and why you are applying for a particular job.

# Long Term Unemployed

If you have never been employed, or it has been many years since you were in employment, the main problem that you will find is explaining the gap in your employment, and demonstrating that you are still employable. At all costs you must avoid giving the prospective employer the impression that you feel hard done by or have a chip on your shoulder.

Employers want to take on positive employees, not those disgruntled and harboring past resentments. At the end of the day, you have a selling job to do and it will be no easy task to convince the employer that you are ready to re-enter the world of work.

## Redundancy

If you have been made redundant, try to show that you understand the company's reasons behind the re-organization. If the organization went out of business, try to show that your attitude towards this was responsible. And do not let the reader of the CV think that this was in any way due to you.

Show that you have somehow learned from the experience by doing something positive which will help you in your future career. If you have undertaken formal training to prepare for a career change or advancement, be specific in how that training fitted the job applied for in the new company.

If you are circulating many unsolicited applications, you must still tailor these to the organizations and the kinds of jobs that you are interested in. Your application is wasted without this. In unsolicited applications, ask if they have any current vacancies for the sort of post that you are seeking. Ask whether their future planning indicates that there may be any available in the near future. Remember to include your most positive points, including the ability to work immediately. This can be a very valuable plus point in your application. .

## Career Breaks

If you have had a career break to raise a family, for example, or are changing career direction it can be very difficult to convince a prospective employer that you are serious about the post and are committed to it. You must convince the employer that you are firmly committed to working and that you have a real interest in their field of work. Cite any refresher courses that you any have taken and emphasize that your childcare arrangements are adequate.

Your career change may be due to circumstances beyond your control. If you have undertaken retraining, sound positive about this and indicate that it was thorough and that you took it seriously. If you are returning to work after a spell in prison, note the Rehabilitation of Offenders Act 1974. This covers people with certain past convictions, but who have not been convicted again for specific lengths of time. After these trouble free periods, the individuals are deemed to have spent their convictions and do not have to declare them. If the conviction has no bearing on your prospective employment and you can avoid mentioning it you should do so. However, you must not lie about it and may have to declare it if asked.

If you are returning to employment in the United Kingdom after working abroad, you must show how the position you held abroad was similar to the kind of job that you had here. The recruiter must be convinced that the change in culture would not mean that your training and abilities have a completely different slant. You may be able to stress the positive side of this too, emphasizing your increased awareness of the international business scene. If you have worked overseas, references may be difficult for the employer to follow up. Testimonials, translated as necessary, may be useful in this situation.

*Now you should read the key points from Chapter Eight overleaf.*

# KEY POINTS FROM CHAPTER EIGHT
## OTHER C.V'S

- If you are a school leaver, keep your CV brief and to the point

- Your education will be the most important part of the CV

- Make a connection between your hobbies and your personal qualities. Try to avoid quoting too many personal interests

- If you are a graduate emphasize your experience (if any) other than your academic experience

- If you are long term unemployed, try to avoid giving the impression that you are disgruntled or resentful

- If you have been made redundant try to portray the redundancy in a positive light. If you have undertaken formal training since being made redundant, be specific in how that training fits the job applied for

- If you have had a career break, you must convince the prospective employer that you are now fully committed to returning to work.

# Covering Letters

# 9

## The ideal covering letter

A covering letter with your CV is really a letter of introduction and is usually the first thing that a prospective employer reads. You should always send a covering letter with a CV or application form. If your application is speculative this is even more important.

The reason for sending the letter is to make sure that the prospective employer has all the facts. Make sure that you keep a copy of what you send.

### Rules of letter writing

Ensure that you use a good quality paper, ideally A4 so that it fits well with other documentation. Do not use colored paper with elaborate designs.

Your letter can be word processed or handwritten as long as the end result is that it is legible. If a person cannot read your letter then they will dispose of it, along with your CV. If you know that your handwriting is bad then word-process the letter. Use black ink for writing letters as this makes it easier for photocopying. The usual rules of spelling and grammar apply in letters as they do in the CV. The overall effect has to convince the reader that they are dealing with a professional.

Any letter that you send must be formal. It must be well set out and show respect to the person that you are writing to. Remember, if you start the letter by saying Dear Sir you must end by saying 'yours faithfully' and that if you use the persons name you must end with 'yours sincerely'. Note that the 'f' and the 's' are in the lower case.

Note how the title of the recipient is given in the advert. If the text asks you to reply to a specific person then you should do just that. Always address the person by their surname and never their forename.

Put your address in the top right hand corner of the letter. You should not put your own name here but leave it until the end of the letter, where you will print and sign. You can, if necessary, put your telephone number under your address. If you put the name and address of the recipient, this should be further down the page on the left hand side. Depending on your style of letter, this date can either be beneath your own address or under the recipients address.

Space the letter out as well as you can. Again, the main rule of letter writing is that the recipient has to get a clear impression of the writer. The more legible the letter, the better laid out, the better the impression. If the letter is short, such as a letter requesting an application form then you should start further down the page.

If there is lots of information in the letter, then you should commence higher up the page. If you can possibly fit it all on one side, then all the better.

Below, you will see an example of a letter forwarding a CV to a prospective employer. Following this, you will see a further two examples. The first one is requesting an application form. The second is returning an application form to a prospective employer.


EXAMPLE 1 OVERLEAF

# Example 1

Daniel Green                    92 Faversham Street
Raft Enterprises               Weybridge
Codley Way                     Surrey
Northampton                    Tel: 020 8123 6789
N1 F45

1st October any date

Dear Mr. Green
**Your Ref: ABCDEFG. Vacancy for a Computer Scientist.**

I would like to apply for the position of computer scientist with your company. I saw the advertisement in the Times in 9th September any date.

As you will see from my enclosed CV, I have been a computer manager since I graduated from Northampton University in 1996. I have been involved in the public and private sectors, overseeing systems analysis and installation.

I believe that I have the experience that you are seeking and would be very interested in working for Raft Enterprises.

I look forward to hearing from you.

Yours sincerely
Rupert James

# Example 2

92 Faversham Street
Weybridge
Surrey

John Baldrick                          Tel: 0208 123 6789
Baldrick Enterprises
Jones Street
Northamption
N1 4RG

1st October any date.

Dear Mr. Baldrick

Your ref: COMP 123. Computer Manager

I am responding to your advertisement in the Times newspaper for a computer scientist. Could you please forward me an application form.

I look forward to hearing from you.

Yours sincerely

Rupert James

**Example 3**

92 Faversham Street
Weybridge
Surrey
020 8 123 6789


Mr. J Baldrick
Baldrick Enterprises
Jones Street
Northampton
N1 4RG

5th October any date

Dear Mr Baldrick

Please find enclosed my application form for the post of computer manager advertised recently in the Times Newspaper.

I look forward to hearing from you soon.

Yours sincerely

Rupert James

## Letters to agencies/consultants

Again, when writing to agencies and consultants, employ exactly the same rules of letter writing but be more specific about what you want if you are writing general letters, not in response to a specific advertisement.

You may wish to give the consultant more information so that he/she can suggest vacancies that you may be interested in applying for. You need to convince the consultant that you are proficient in your chosen field. Therefore, your application must look professional. Remember that it will go from the consultant to a number of companies.

The golden rule throughout letter writing is that a letter must be laid out on quality paper, well written, clear and to the point.

*Now read the key points from chapter nine overleaf.*

# KEY POINTS FROM CHAPTER NINE
# COVERING LETTERS

- Always send a covering letter with a CV or application form

- Always use good quality paper

- Always type your letter if your handwriting is not so good

- Letters must always be formal, never familiar

- Spend time laying out your letter. Double-check it when you finish

  - Be brief and be clear!

# Application Forms

# 10

## Application forms

---

If you are applying for a job that requires you to fill an application form in, there are several important rules to remember. When you receive the form never fill in the original in the first instance. You might make a mistake and not be happy with what you have written and might need to start again. By then, if you are using the original, it will be too late. Always copy the form and fill it in with a pencil. This way, you will not suffer if you make a mistake.

Application forms can either be written or typed. It is up to you to exercise your discretion at this point. However, only if your handwriting is neat should you fill in the form by hand. A typewritten form will be more immediately readable and make a better first impression.

Send the application form in with a brief covering letter. Do not falsify the application form, as this will form part of your contract of employment when offered the post.

The job application should be treated much the same way as your CV. As we discussed, when you interpret the job advertisement you need to analyze the nature of the job before compiling the CV. You should do exactly the same with an application form. The first task is to read the job description that should normally accompany the application form.

It is absolutely essential that you understand the requirements of the post. Many organizations will send a person specification that outlines the essential and desirable criteria, which the applicant must meet before he or she is considered for the post. Although the essential criteria are the most important, if those short listing for the post have a number of good candidates then they will revert to the desirable criteria as a way of further eliminating candidates.

It follows that, when completing an application form, which has a person specification in it, then you should fill in the application carefully following the requirements of the post, ensuring that you meet the essential and desirable criteria. In addition to essential and desirable criteria, there will be a skills required section, which will generally outline the skills and abilities, which the person must demonstrate.

Make sure that when you fill in your application form that you follow the person specification closely, you have read and understood the job description and that you comply with all the requirements. If you do not, then you are wasting your time.

Normally, there is a space on an application form, which asks you to outline your experience to date and to demonstrate why you want the job. You should be concise and to the point. On too many application forms, applicants really go to town in this section, producing a whole life history amounting to many sides of paper. This is totally unnecessary and will, more often that not, result in your application being thrown in the bin.

You should follow carefully the requirements of the post, from the person specification to the job description, and lay out clearly and concisely your experience to date. You should then relate this to the job on offer and explain why you think that you are the ideal candidate.

If there is no job description or person specification to work from, then you will need to read very carefully the requirements of the post from the advertisement, and then construct what you think are the main aspects of the job related to your own experience. In this way, you can present the interviewer with a picture of yourself. It is not very often these days that an application form is not accompanied by a job description.

If you feel that you are on uncertain ground, for example when faced with filling in an application form without a job description or person specification, then you might want to contact the company concerned and request further information.

## Content of application forms

The application form will proceed on a logical progressive basis, much as a CV is compiled. The form will start by asking you your name and address, some will ask your date of birth. The type of organization that you are applying to will very much determine the application you are being asked to fill in.

Some application forms are designed with great care and reflect the ethos of the organization, such as omitting to ask certain information on an equal opportunities ground. For example, some organizations deliberately do not ask for information relating to age as this is thought to affect the perceptions of those who are short listing for the post.

There will be a space for a phone number. This is important, as the company may want to contact you by phone shortly after the interview to discuss the possibilities of offering you a job.

Other details at the beginning of an application form might be sex, marital status and country and place of birth. This again will vary depending on the organization you are applying to. The next section of the form will ask you for details of education. You should start with your most recent job first. However, it is very important to read the application form as it might state otherwise.

Applications might ask for salary information and reasons for leaving the post. As discussed, on a CV it is not wise to volunteer this information, with the exception of final salary. However, some application forms may require this and will say so.

If the state of your health has not involved disability but has involved long periods off work then you should try to demonstrate to your employer that this problem is now in the past and that this will not affect your future employment.

Most applications end by asking for references. These will normally be from your current employer and one other, such as someone who has known you for a long time. If you are not currently employed then the reference should be from your ex-employer. Make sure that you know what your employer or ex employer is going to say about you in advance. It follows that you should let this person know that you are going to use them as a reference.

Many employers do not bother taking up references despite asking for them. Others always take them up as a matter of course. Some applications state that they will take up references when a candidate is short-listed. You should contact the company and state that you do not want this ads it could affect your relationship with your employer (if this is the case).

If you have not yet been employed then you should use school or academic references. A second reference might be a personal reference. Some applications will ask specifically for a personal reference. In this case, it is better to use a professional reference, i.e. someone with whom you have worked in a voluntary capacity or even someone you have worked in a paid capacity for.

There are a number of other questions that may appear on an application form, such as whether or not you have a driving license or whether you speak any other languages. Notice periods, possible start dates and periods of notice, plus membership of professional bodies may also appear.

There may also be a requirement to outline your ambitions. Be careful and tailor this to your employer's requirements.

*Now you should read the key points from chapter ten overleaf.*

# KEY POINTS FROM CHAPTER TEN
# APPLICATION FORMS

- Always fill in a copy of the original application form. Use a pencil to do this. Only when you are happy with the original product should you transfer it to the original.

- You should always type the form unless your handwriting is very neat.

- Send the form with a brief covering letter.

- Read the job description and person specification carefully. Fill the form in following the requirements of the post.

- Be concise and keep to the point, particularly in the experience to date section of the form.

- If there is no job description and person specification, and you are in doubt, then you should contact the company concerned and request more details.

- Check with potential referees before using them.

# Other tips

# 11

# Where and how to send your CV

---

It is true to say that companies are always in the process of recruiting, even in these straitened times. Most companies, particularly the bigger ones will experience a fairly high turnover of staff per annum. Companies therefore have vacancies and it is imperative that your CV is available to view at the right moment.

There are a number of ways to distribute your CV other than the time-honored method of forwarding it direct to the employer when a vacancy is advertised. Below, we look at the most effective ways. In appendix one there are a number of Internet sites listed to which you can send your CV.

## Distribution of your CV through the internet

There are two main forms of electronic CV distribution through the Internet:

- Posting your CV in CV banks, which are searched by corporate recruiters and also headhunters

- Sending your CV direct to an employers website.

## CV banks

There are a lot of CV banks where your CV can be posted for free. A search online, merely tapping in the words CV bank will bring up sites. Most of these sites have standardized CV forms which you must fill in. Every time you post a CV online in this way it will be seen by a lot of potential employers. These banks are periodically cleaned out, every three months or so, so make a note of when a CV was posted.

## Employers web sites

Posting your CV to individual employers web sites obviously takes longer than posting it to a CV bank but it is more direct and is guaranteed to reach your target. Most employers web sites have a recruitment section where the posting can take place. Again, company databases are purged at frequent intervals so it is up to you to monitor the situation.

## Newspapers

Many people still use this tried and tested route, mass mailing of CV's to many companies. It is advisable to check that you are buying the right target paper for your own desired area of employment. For example, the guardian has main days, usually Tuesday and Wednesday when it advertises a whole range of jobs, from media to education to housing to social work. It is important to identify which day is appropriate for you and also to see in the adverts whether CV's are acceptable. Not all companies or prospective employers accept CV's.

## Employment agencies

There are many agencies in the market place all competing for work. Many agencies are specialist, specializing in certain types of skillsets, i.e. construction, driving, social work, housing, secretarial and so on.

You should identify the list of agencies appropriate to you and send a copy of your updated CV to them. They will then contact you and, usually, ask you to come in for an interview. Many will ask if it is OK to take up references and some will take up a CRB (criminal records) check, depending on the type of work being undertaken.

## Vocational and college placement offices

Obviously, if you are a student and have access to this resource then it is essential that you make use of it.

101

## Business and trade publications

Many trades and businesses have their own publications and often will advertise jobs in these. The construction industry and social work plus housing sectors all have their own journals. A library is a good place to start with narrowing down specific journals.

## The importance of following up

Having made a big effort in producing your CV and then having, one way or another, sent it to prospective employers, it is essential that you follow up your efforts. If you don't do this then it is highly likely that your CV will sit in some busy person's in-tray for ages. A call to the appropriate person in human resources (personnel) will at least get you known to the company and may move you a few notches up the ladder.

# Interviews

# 12

## The interview stage and pre-interview tests

Having sent in your C.V or sent in your application form, at some point there will be a response, usually inviting you for an interview. Some firms will, on your arrival, ask you to sit a test. This should not usually be a surprise, as you will normally receive advance notice in the letter inviting you for an interview. It is advisable to know something about the nature of these tests before you arrive for the interview.

Therefore, before a more general discussion about interviews, it is necessary to discuss the range of tests that an employer may want you to carry out before or during the interview stage. The most common are known as psychological or psychometric tests. Not all interviews are preceded by a test of this sort, but they are becoming common enough to warrant a discussion in order to give an idea of what may be faced.

A psychometric test is simply a standard way of measuring some specific attribute or aspect of mental behavior. It is standard because everyone who does a particular test is treated in exactly the same way, as are the results. The idea is to produce an objective summary of what a person is or is not good at and how they come across as an individual.

There are literally thousands of different tests on the market, measuring a whole different range of attributes. Most measure one or other of the following:

- Attainment. Your learnt ability, for example what you know about arithmetic or spelling

- Aptitude. Your ability to acquire further knowledge or skills for example your understanding of words or ideas

- Personality. What you are like as a person, for example, are you outgoing or quiet and thoughtful?

- Values. What you think is important, for example money or power, or both

- Interests. What would you liker to do or what activities do you think would suit you best? For example, would you prefer to fell trees or write newspaper articles

- Skills. What you have learnt to do practically, for example there are standard tests for differing occupations.

Psychometric tests require you to answer all the questions and there is only one correct answer. You are not expected to finish in the time allowed, thereby distinguishing tests from exams. Tests can measure lots of separate abilities of which the most common are:

- Verbal ability

- Numerical ability

- Perceptual ability (understanding and reasoning)

- Spatial ability. How well you picture shapes being moved in three dimensions

- Mechanical ability

- Abstract ability. How well you can analyze a problem.

- Clerical ability. How well you understand simple arithmetic and use of English.

All these tests can be used by themselves or in combination. There are also tests for people with different levels of ability, such as those specially designed for graduates or managers.

## Personality tests

The ancient Greeks arrived at four basic personality tests and in the twentieth century, scientists have refined these as follows:

- Extrovert-introvert
- Confident-anxious
- Structured-non structured
- Conformist-non-conformist

Personality tests attempt to measure where you come on these scales.

## Preparing for tests

Although your early life will prepare you for tests, there are certain things that you can do to improve your performance. You should ensure that:

- You have some information on your potential employer on the sort of thing that you will be doing.

- Have an understanding what testing is like, what the experience is like.

There are many books on the market ranging from personality to I.Q tests. It is worth investing in such a book, or visiting your local library and spend some time doing a few selected tests.

To ensure that everyone has an equal chance to do their best, most tests are administered under carefully controlled conditions. This means that you complete the tests sitting at a desk facing a test administrator. As many tests are given to groups, you will find yourself sitting in a row, schoolroom fashion with other candidates. The test administrator will:

- Welcome you and introduce him/herself.

- Explain the purpose of the test.

- Detail the nature of the tests.

- Explain how the tests are to be administered.

Although most personality tests are un-timed, you are expected to finish in a reasonable time, about 35-45 minutes.

The test administrator will:
- Read out instructions for the test.

- Ask you to complete some practice questions and/or explain some worked examples.

- Tell you how much time you have for the test.

- Stop the test when appropriate and introduce the next one.

- Close the session and give you some information on what will happen next.

## Assessment of tests

With ability tests, the employer will look to see how many questions have been answered correctly. This gives you what is known as the raw score. Your raw score is then standardized using something called a normative group. This is a large representative sample of people who have done the test in the past, including current jobholders, graduates, managers and the general population, among others.

When scores have been standardized they can be compared on an objective basis with other peoples, and employers can see if you have scored above or below average and also how much above or below.

Personality tests operate in a slightly different way because there are no right or wrong answers. However, comparisons can be made within a normative group and allow employers to see, for example, if you are more or less extroverted that the average person.

Once standardized, test results can be used in one of two ways: as a source of information, which can be used at interview or as a screening device. When results are used to screen candidate's two further selection techniques can be used: top down or minimum cut off.

Top down means that candidates are picked on the basis of highest scores leading down. Minimum cut off selects everyone who scores over a set level.

Again, personality tests are different since it makes no sense to use top down or minimum cut off. However, candidates may be selected out if they score at the wrong extreme on a critical dimension.

If you have been tested and have been unsuccessful at this stage then the employer will always usually be prepared to give you feedback on your tests. This can often be very useful.

It is now time to discuss interviews generally. Not all employers will give you a test and, as stated, often tests are carried out prior to undertaking the interview.

# The interview

You do not get to the interview stage unless the employer believes that you can do the job. This means that you have already been accepted on the basis of your C.V or application. You supply all the information about yourself. This means that while the interviewer controls the structure of the interview, decisions can only be made on the basis of what you provide.

Most of the interview questions can be predicted in advance. This being the case, you can prepare answers in your own time, which cast you in the most positive light.

Before we look at interview tactics, it is useful to know that there are a number of different types of interview. There are three main variations:

- Single. This is a one to one meeting between the interviewer and candidate. Of all the types of interview, it is the most relaxing for both interviewer and interviewee alike. This type of interview is favored by smaller organizations although there can be a potential for bias.

- Sequential interview. This is where there is a series of interviews, usually two or maybe three, carried out by different interviewers. It allows for a range of impressions to be gathered.

Although in theory this process should be more democratic, in practice the most senior interviewer will have the most sway

.

- Panel interview. This involves being questioned by a number of interviewers, in turn at the same interview. This type of interview is popular in most organizations and the number of interviewers varies. The type of person interviewing will vary depending on the type of organization.

## The facts about interviews

The latest figures show that 90% of organizations use interviews. Interviewers will make up their mind quite rapidly, usually after the first four or five minutes. Making a positive first impression is very important indeed. Different interviewers set different standards. They pay attention to information that is out of the ordinary and are more influenced by negative information than positive.

Interviewers are not very good at assessing real personality. This is not really possible in such a short space of time. Characteristics often begin to manifest themselves several weeks into the job. How you are judged during and after an interview depends very much on whom the interviewer has seen. This is known technically as the Halo effect.

There are many other points about interviews, one main one being that subjectivity will creep in, i.e. how well your face fits, whether you are considered to be a team player and so on. At the end of the day you have to fit into the organization and those interviewing will only employ you if this is perceived to be the case.

## Preparing for interviews

Although some of the negative aspects of the interview process have been stressed, you should always try to be positive. You need to pay a lot of attention to preparing for the interview. A few preliminary points need to be considered:

- Do you know exactly where and what time the interview is taking place. This may sound silly, but in your initial excitement and haste, you may overlook it until the last moment and may find yourself at a disadvantage.

- Do you know who is going to be interviewing you, their name and job title?

- Do you know enough about the organization, have you researched them and do you know enough about their history and product?

## Presentation

This is of the utmost importance. What you wear will have to be appropriate to the type of business you are dealing with. You are going to a business meeting so you should wear the smartest clothes that you can and dress conservatively. Dark colors shave a greater impact. The main point here is that you should not disadvantage yourself, no matter what your outlook on life. You may secretly hate wearing a suit and tie but in order to get the job you want you have to bend to the whims of the employer. Remember, they have the power in this situation and you have to prove yourself.

## Materials

Don't forget to take your C.V or application to the interview. Also take a pen and paper for taking notes. Prepare some questions to ask the interviewers when the interview is over.

There is nothing worse than saying that you have no questions. This disappoints the interviewers and leads them to think that you are not very interested in their organization.

## Making an Impression

As mentioned, research has shown that interviewers usually make up their minds during the first few minutes and spend the rest of the interview trying to confirm this impression.

First impressions are based on several things: what you look like and how you behave. The impression that you make will, to a large degree, depend on the interviewer and his or her prejudices and dislikes and overall bias.

## Body language

This bit will require some practice. Obviously, your body language will vary depending on the situation you are in, those in front of you and how you feel at the time. The impression that you will make will rest on:

- Facial expression and how you move your head.

- What you do with your hands and arms.

- What you do with the rest of your body.

It is also useful to know that, in terms of being believable, the most accurate signals someone gives out are such things as going pale, swallowing and sweating, which are automatic, followed by what you do with your legs and feet and the rest of your body. A few important points:

- Look at the interviewer and smile.

- Keep your hands away from your face.

- Nod your head to show that you are paying attention.

- Lean forward when speaking and back when listening.

*At the same time:*

- Do not make sudden movements.

- Do not fold your arms.

In particular, sit in a relaxed manner and do not fidget. This means do not move about on the seat and keep your feet and hands still.

You need to give the interviewer the impression of being business like and confident, genuinely interested in the position on offer.

## The structure of the interview

At the outset, the interviewer will try to relax you and break the ice. An effort will be made to explain the interview process to you. There is a fairly common format to the interview process and this will normally tie in to the C.V or application form.

The interviewer will begin by talking about the organization and its history and future plans. Then you will be invited to tell the interviewer(s) about your own recent work history and how it fits in with the job on offer. They may even ask you at this stage why you have applied for the post although this normally comes later.

Generally, the questions related to the post will begin at this time. The interviewers will ask you structured questions. Usually, candidates for a job will get asked the same questions. This, however, will vary depending on the post, the organization and other factors.

At the end of the questions you will normally be told about the terms and conditions, and also about the interview process, i.e. when they expect to be able to make a decision.

There are many variations on the above theme. During the course of the interview, the person(s) interviewing may decide to concentrate more on you and ask you about your aspirations.

You should always be cautious here and appear ambitious but not unrealistic. If your employer thinks that they cannot meet your aspirations then it may cost you your job.

They may try to gauge your interests and your circumstances in order to build up a clearer picture of you and try to get a picture of your background.

This very much depends on the job and interviewers. It is the practice in the public sector, for example, to try to remain as objective as possible, also in larger private sector organizations. However, this may differ radically in other organizations depending on size, nature of the operation and so on.

There are a few golden rules in interviews. Never get too aggressive or arrogant in front of the interviewers. This can happen for a number of reasons. It can be down to nervousness, insecurity or the fact that you are doing badly, or at least you feel you are and try to mask this by being hostile or aggressive.

If you fall into this mode of behavior then you will almost certainly not get the job. If you feel that you cannot answer a question then you should ask the person to go back to it later. This will give you more time to focus your mind and relax.

Earlier, we talked about preparation. Part of preparation is mental preparation. Putting you into the right frame of mind and becoming confident.

If you stop to think about it, all you are doing is sitting in front of people who work for a firm, who wish you no harm and want to see you succeed. If you think yourself into this frame of mind, then even if you get the idea that you are not doing well then you can still retain your self-confidence and dignity.

## How do interviewers make decisions?

A good interviewer will assess you against the requirements for the job. This means that your particular skills, abilities, experiences and knowledge will be matched against a list of essential and desirable qualities. It might be that a particular sort of business experience is required and ideally the employer is seeking certain types of qualifications. The list is known as the person specification, and the better the fit between you and the person specification the greater the chances of getting the job.

This makes it sound simple, in reality however the process is quite complicated. The reason for this is that certain sorts of information appear to be more influential than others. The following factors are seen to be particularly influential:

- Personality. How you present yourself as a person.

- Experience. The experience you have that is relevant to the job.

- Qualifications. The qualifications that you have which are relevant to the job.

- Background. Your general work background and your track record.

- Enthusiasm. How motivated and interested you appear to be about the job.

- Education. Your general level of educational experience.

This list reinforces the critical need to make a powerful and positive impression on the employer. It also stresses the need to relate experience, qualifications and general work background to the job in question and give the impression that you are an energetic and motivated individual with a genuine interest in the work and the employer's organization.

Whatever the method of assessing the information or the weight given to it, the end result is that you will eventually be offered a job or turned down. This process takes time and during this period another part of the selection system comes into operation. The employer will offer the job to the best candidate but the second or even the third will not be rejected. Someone is always kept in reserve in case the first candidate rejects the job offer.

In general, if you have not heard anything after ten days, contact the employer and ask if a decision has been made. Sometimes, people are actually offered a job at the interview. If this happens to you, remember that it could mean a number of things:

- The employer is very impressed.

- You have undersold yourself.

- The employer is desperate

In relation to underselling yourself, you should leave all salary negotiations to the end of the selection process. If you are asked what you expect to be paid, give a range and ask what the rate for the job is. The point is that you are in a much more powerful negotiating position when someone actually wants you and genuinely believes that you are the best person for the job.

## Reading the signs

Before the final decision, you can get some indication of your performance if you consider what happened at the interview. Positive signs include:

- Any detailed discussions about salary.

- Any exploration of when you can start the job.

- An interview that lasts longer than expected.

- An interview, which includes unscheduled meetings with other decision makers, such as managers.

- Being invited to a second interview.

In contrast, negative signs are:
- An interview, which is much shorter than anticipated, perhaps only 20 minutes long.

- Being repeatedly caught out by the interviewer and not being able to answer the questions.
- An obvious clash between your personal requirements and what the company can provide, for example in terms of work hours.

After the interview, if you have been turned down, you should contact the company and try to get feedback form the interview. This can be invaluable and put you on the right track for the next interview.

*Now read the key points from Chapter Twelve overleaf.*

# KEY POINTS FROM CHAPTER TWELVE
# THE INTERVIEW STAGE AND PRE-INTERVIEW TESTS

- It is advisable to know something about pre-interview/interview tests before the interview stage.

- The most common tests are psychological and psychometric tests.

- Psychometric tests measure lots of abilities, most commonly verbal, numerical, perceptual, spatial, mechanical, abstract and clerical abilities.

- Personality tests measure the nature of your personality, i.e., extrovert, introvert, confidence etc.

- Most interview questions can be predicted in advance. You should prepare thoroughly by rehearsing possible questions.

- Always present the best side of yourself and be as relaxed as possible.

- Always be prepared and take your C.V or application form.

# Final comments

As you have seen, throughout this book the emphasis has been on care and quality, beginning with the interpretation of the job advert through to compiling your C.V and attending the interview.

The most important elements are:

- Be professional-take care with your presentation

- Believe in yourself

- Do not be put off by failure.

This will ensure that you are in with a fighting chance of getting the job that you want.

Good Luck!

# Internet sites for jobseekers

As we have discussed, it is becoming more common to send CV's and also to glean job information over the internet. The below represents some of the best sites.

1. www.jobs.guardian.co.uk

This site has many new jobs every day. Jobs are sorted by type and it is easy to search for jobs that are relevant to your needs. You can complete a profile on this site to which your CV can be attached. This can then be made available to specific employers who might be in interested in you. There is no charge for this service. You can also upload your CV so that it can be sent to any vacancy advertised.

2. www.ft.com

This is the Financial Times Recruitment site, specialising particularly in the financial sector.

3. www.timesonline.co.uk

This is the website of the Times newspaper group, which contains their job pages. The site includes CV tips and useful guidelines.

4. www.jobs.co.uk

This particular site links to employers' websites so that you can apply for a job directly.

5. www.reed.co.uk

This site is owned by Reed employment who are a well known employment agency. As befits employments agencies, it includes many tips and useful guidance on CV compilation, job searching, interviews etc.

6. www.bradleyscvs.co.uk

This is a well known website that offers CV writing services for free. It is a very useful site indeed for those who are involved in CV compilation for the first time.

Other useful sites

**General vacancies**

www.jobtrack.co.uk

www.peoplebank.co.uk

www.topjobs.co.uk

www.ukjobbs.com
Monster Job Search Online : www.monster.co.uk

Search The Top UK JOBS: www.j-ojobs.com

Find Job Vacancies in your Area: www.cv-library.co.uk

**Voluntary work sites**

www.jobseekers.direct.gov.uk

This is the UK government's main portal to all sorts of jobs, training and volunteering opportunities.

www.jobcentreplus.gov.uk

The UK government's job website.

www.volunteering.org.uk

This site is run by volunteering England and usually has many opportunities.

## Other general sites

Royal British legion (ex servicemen and women)
www.rbli.co.uk
General business directory: www.ukbusinesspark.co.uk
Confederation of British Industry www.cbi.org.uk

# Index

Easyway Guides
Brighton BN7 2SH

If you would like to know more about the Easyway Guides
Series, or would like to write for us please contact us at:
info@straightforwardco.co.uk or phone

01273 472982